The Book of Machine Learning

Abeer Verma

Fusion Books

Publisher	:	**Fusion Books** X-30, Okhla Industrial Area, Phase-II New Delhi-110020
Phone	:	011- 40712200
E-mail	:	wecare@diamondbooks.in
Website	:	www.diamondbooks.in
Edition	:	2026

Author's Note

Hi, I'm Abeer Verma — a Grade 11 student who became curious about Machine Learning not because it was trending, but because I kept wondering how my phone knew my face and how apps seemed to understand my choices.

At first, I assumed Machine Learning was something only scientists or big tech companies worked on. The term itself sounded complicated. But when I began exploring beginner tools and reading about how models learn from patterns, I realized something important — the core idea is actually simple and logical.

What surprised me most was that Machine Learning isn't just about coding. It's about observation, curiosity, experimentation, and asking the right questions. It's about understanding patterns — something we already do naturally as students.

This book reflects my learning journey so far. I've written it in the way I would explain these ideas to my classmates — clearly, practically, and without unnecessary jargon. I am still learning, and that's exactly why I wanted to write this: to show that you don't have to be an expert to start understanding how machines learn.

My hope is that after reading this book, you won't just see Machine Learning as something complex or distant. Instead, you'll see it as something you can explore, question, and even build with.
If a high school student can begin this journey, so can you.

— Abeer Verma
Grade 11 Student

Preface

Dear Young Explorer,
Welcome to the world where machines learn just like you do—by seeing, trying, making mistakes, and improving.
When I first started reading about Machine Learning, I expected it to be full of complicated formulas and advanced programming. Instead, I discovered that at its core, Machine Learning is about something very simple: learning from examples and patterns.

From recommending your favorite song to helping doctors diagnose diseases faster, Machine Learning (ML) is everywhere. But what is it really? How does a robot "learn"? Can you build your own ML project?

These were the same questions I had when I began exploring this field. The answers, I realized, are not limited to research labs or big tech companies—they are accessible to students who are curious enough to explore.
This book, The Book of Machine Learning, is written for curious young minds who want to understand how the smart technology around them actually works.

It is written keeping in mind India's vision of future-ready education under NEP 2020, where students are encouraged to think critically, build practical skills, and connect learning to real-world challenges. Each chapter follows a simple "5Ws" approach—What, Why, When, Where, Who—so that you don't just memorize definitions, but actually understand the bigger picture. You'll find real-life Indian

examples, relatable stories, hands-on tools, and reflection questions to help you think deeper.
I’ve tried to explain concepts the way I would explain them to my classmates—clearly, practically, and without unnecessary technical complexity.

Whether you dream of being a coder, an artist, a gamer, a teacher, or a changemaker, ML can empower your path.
My goal is not just to teach you what Machine Learning is, but to help you feel confident enough to experiment with it yourself.
So read on, explore the illustrations, try out tools like Teachable Machine or Scratch ML, and most importantly—stay curious.
Let’s move beyond seeing Machine Learning as “smart technology” and start seeing it as something we can understand, question, and build responsibly.
Let’s unlock the logic behind machines that learn.

With curiosity and excitement,
Abeer Verma

INDEX

Chapter 1

What Is Machine Learning, Really?

Welcome to the World of Learning Machines!

Imagine a world where your phone knows which photo you're likely to tap, your shopping app predicts what snack you might crave, and your voice assistant says, "Good morning!" just when you wake up. Sounds like magic? It's actually Machine Learning—a powerful technology that helps machines learn from data and make smart decisions.

But here's the big question:
What exactly is Machine Learning?
Can machines really learn?
Is it something only scientists do—or can you learn and build it too?
In this chapter, we'll dive into the exciting world of ML using fun examples, real-life stories, and simple ideas that will stick with you forever.
Let's begin by imagining this...

A Robot Learns to Sort Toys

Meet Aanya, a 13-year-old student from Jaipur who loves robots. One day, she decides to teach her robot friend, Botu, to clean her messy toy room.

She has three boxes:

- One for cars
- One for animals
- One for blocks

She shows Botu 50 pictures of each toy type and labels them.

Botu begins to learn:

Cars have wheels.
Animals have ears or tails.
Blocks are colorful and square.

Soon, when Aanya drops a toy on the floor, Botu can say, "That's a car!" and put it in the correct box—all by itself.

That's Machine Learning in action!

So, What Is Machine Learning?

Let's define it clearly.
Machine Learning (ML) is a type of technology that allows computers to learn from data and experience—without being told what to do step by step.
Just like you learn from mistakes and practice, machines can learn from examples.

Here's an everyday example:

- **Without ML:** A spam filter blocks emails that contain words like "Congratulations" or "Win money"—because someone programmed those rules.

• **With ML:** A spam filter sees thousands of spam and non-spam emails and learns to recognize spam on its own, even if the words change.

In short:

YOU Learn From	MACHINES Learn From
Books, teachers, experiences	Data, examples, patterns

Why Is ML Called "Learning"?

Because it mimics how humans learn.

Let's say you're learning to recognize a mango:

1. Someone shows you a few mangoes.
2. You see the color, shape, size.
3. Next time you see a mango, your brain says, "Aha! Mango!"

ML works the same way.
The machine is shown lots of examples and eventually learns to make a good guess.
It's not magic. It's not copying. It's pattern recognition!

ML vs. Traditional Programming

Let's compare:

Feature	Traditional Programming	Machine Learning
Based on	Rules written by humans	Data learned from examples
Example	If marks > 90 → grade A	Learn how to grade by analyzing 1,000 report cards

Flexibility	Can't handle new situations well	Learns and improves over time
Coding	Must code every rule	Code teaches the machine how to learn

The 5Ws of Machine Learning

Let's break ML down using the 5Ws Framework—a powerful way to understand any concept.

1. What is Machine Learning?
It's the science of helping computers learn patterns and make decisions by themselves using data.
Think of ML as teaching a friend to recognize your handwriting—not by memorizing, but by practicing with samples.

2. Why is Machine Learning Important Today?
We are surrounded by massive amounts of data—videos, photos, texts, health records, shopping history, GPS movement, and more.

Humans cannot process all of it manually. ML helps by:
- Speeding up decisions
- Personalizing experiences
- Solving big problems like disease prediction, climate analysis, and crop planning

It's like having a super assistant working behind the scenes.

3. When & Where is ML Used?
ML is used every single moment, often without us realizing it.

Here are some places:

Area	How ML Helps
Phones	Unlock with face, predict emojis

Games	Adjust difficulty based on your skill
Shopping	Suggest items based on your taste
Maps	Recommend fastest routes using traffic data
Schools	Personalize lessons to your learning speed
Banks	Detect fraud and secure accounts
Hospitals	Analyze X-rays, predict disease risk
Farming	Predict rainfall, detect plant diseases

Even Google Translate, ChatGPT, and Instagram filters use ML!

4. Who Uses ML?

Creators:
- Data scientists
- Software engineers
- Students like you using beginner tools!

Users:
- Teachers
- Doctors
- Farmers
- YOU!

ML is for everyone, not just for people in big labs or tech companies.

5. How Does It Work? (More in Chapter 2)

Quick sneak peek:
- Collect data
- Feed it to a model (like a brain for the machine)
- The model finds patterns
- Machine starts making predictions

It's like feeding a pet new treats and watching it learn tricks!

Real-Life Story: ML at Home

Riya's parents installed a smart home assistant. At first, it didn't recognize her voice.

But every day, Riya used it to say:
"Turn on the light."
"Play dance music."
"What's the weather?"
After a week, it began to understand her voice, accent, and choice of words.
Riya didn't program it. She just taught it. That's the beauty of ML.

Illustration Prompt

Scene Idea:
A girl (Aanya) standing next to her robot in a toy-filled room.
Three boxes: "Cars," "Animals," "Blocks."
The robot is looking at a toy with a glowing light above its head showing "Learning..."
Background filled with books, laptop, and thought bubbles like "Pattern," "Color," "Shape."

Did You Know?

• In 1997, IBM's computer "Deep Blue" defeated the world chess champion—the first time a machine beat a human in chess!
• Netflix saves over $1 billion a year using ML to recommend shows you're likely to enjoy!
• India's CropIn is an AI-powered app helping farmers make better decisions using weather + soil data + satellite images.

Let's Play: "Is It ML or Not?"

Instructions: Read each example and say whether it uses ML.

1. A calculator adds 123 + 45 →
2. Your phone unlocks when it sees your face →
3. You type "B" in Google, and it suggests "Birthday Wishes in Hindi" →
4. A washing machine turns off after 30 minutes →

Answers:

1. ✗ Not ML (just calculation)
2. ✓ Yes, face recognition uses ML
3. ✓ Yes, autocomplete uses ML
4. ✗ No, it's a timer (no learning involved)

Activity: Your ML Diary

Start a mini-diary called:
"My Encounters with Machine Learning"
Every day for 5 days, write 2 times ML helped you.

Example:
• "YouTube suggested a video I actually liked!"
• "My typing app corrected my spelling."
You'll be amazed how often you meet ML!

Career Spotlight

Data Scientist

• Builds models from data
• Works with numbers, trends, and tools
• Helps companies improve products and services
• Needs math, curiosity, coding, and communication skills

Tip: Start learning Python and explore free courses on YouTube or government portals like AI For Youth by CBSE.

India Shining: ML in Our Country

• Aarogya Setu App used ML to track COVID spread and alert users.
• CropIn and SatSure use ML to help farmers monitor crop health.
• NITI Aayog is promoting ML learning in schools under Atal Tinkering Labs.

India is not just using ML—we're shaping its future!

Think & Reflect

1. Can a machine really "understand" like a human? Why or why not?
2. If you could teach a robot one thing, what would it be?
3. Is ML always accurate? What if it makes a mistake?

Abeer's Quick Tip

When you first hear terms like "Machine Learning" or "models," don't try to memorize definitions. Pick one real-life example—like face unlock or YouTube recommendations—and trace how it might work step by step. Understanding one example deeply is better than skimming ten concepts quickly.

Chapter Recap

• Machine Learning means teaching machines to learn from data and patterns.

- It is everywhere—in your phone, school, games, and government!
- ML is not only for tech experts. Even kids can start with beginner tools!
- The 5Ws help you understand ML deeply: What, Why, When, Where, Who.
- The future of ML is exciting—and you're a part of it.

Chapter 2

How Does Machine Learning Actually Work? (Data Patterns Prediction)

Let's Go Behind the Scenes

In the last chapter, you learned that Machine Learning is about teaching machines to learn from data. But how does that happen? How does a machine go from being a blank slate to a smart assistant that recommends movies or recognizes your face?

In this chapter, we'll break down the process of Machine Learning into simple steps. Don't worry—we won't throw big, scary equations at you. Instead, we'll use fun examples, beginner tools, and a lot of imagination.

Let's begin with a story.

Meet Aryan and Robo

Aryan is a 14-year-old student from Hyderabad who loves robotics and football. He built a robot named RoboCoach to help him train better.

His goal? To make RoboCoach say:
• "Good shot!" when the ball goes into the net.
• "Try again!" when the shot misses.

But how does RoboCoach learn what's a goal and what's not?

Here's how Aryan trained it:
1. He recorded 100 kicks and labeled them as "goal" or "miss."
2. He fed that data into RoboCoach's system.
3. RoboCoach analyzed the patterns (like ball speed, direction, kick angle).
4. Then, it started making predictions on new kicks.

That's the secret of ML:
Data → Learn Patterns → Make Predictions

Let's unpack this step by step.

Step 1: Data – The Fuel of Machine Learning

Think of data as the food your machine brain eats.
The more healthy, diverse, and well-prepared the food (data), the smarter your machine becomes.

Types of Data
• **Text:** Chat messages, emails, captions
• **Images:** Photos, drawings, screenshots
• **Numbers:** Test scores, prices, temperatures
• **Sound:** Voice commands, music
• **Videos:** Recordings, surveillance footage

Real-Life Analogy:
Just like your brain needs different experiences to learn—reading, listening, observing—a machine also learns better from diverse data.

Step 2: Labeling – Tagging the Examples

This is called "Supervised Learning", where you show the machine examples along with correct answers.

Example:

Image	Label
	Dog
	Cat
	Dog

Just like a teacher corrects your homework, you correct the machine's guesses—until it starts guessing right on its own.

Step 3: Patterns – Spotting the Hidden Clues

Once the machine has data, it starts looking for patterns.

For instance, it might discover:

- All photos labeled "cat" have pointy ears and whiskers.
- Emails marked as "spam" often say "free" or "win now."

This part is like the machine playing "Spot the Difference" a thousand times until it gets really good at it!

Fun Metaphor:
Imagine your ML model is a detective. You give it a bunch of clues (data), and it starts solving the mystery by figuring out what traits match with what result.

Step 4: Prediction – The Machine Makes a Guess

Once trained, your machine is ready to make decisions on new, unseen data.

Let's say Aryan kicks the ball again.

RoboCoach has never seen this exact shot before—but it analyzes the speed, angle, and motion, and says:

"Good shot!"
Even if RoboCoach has never seen this exact kick, it has seen enough similar ones to make a smart prediction.

From My Experience

When I first tried building a small ML model using image classification, my model kept giving wrong predictions. Later I realized the lighting in my room was uneven, and I had not provided enough examples. That's when I understood how important "good data" really is.

Quick Summary of ML Workflow

Let's visualize the steps as a flowchart:

css
CopyEdit
Collect Data → Clean and Label It → Feed to ML Model → Model Learns Patterns → Makes Predictions → Improves with Feedback

It's like a learning loop—just like how you improve in studies with practice and corrections.

Try It Yourself: Teachable Machine by Google

Tool Spotlight: TeachableMachine.withGoogle.com

What it does:
You can teach your computer to recognize images, sounds, or poses—no coding needed!

How to use it:

1. Visit the website.
2. Choose what you want to teach: image, sound, or pose.
3. Upload or record examples (e.g., smile vs. frown).
4. Click "Train Model."
5. Test it live using your webcam or mic!

In just 10 minutes, you've trained your own ML model!

Illustration Prompt

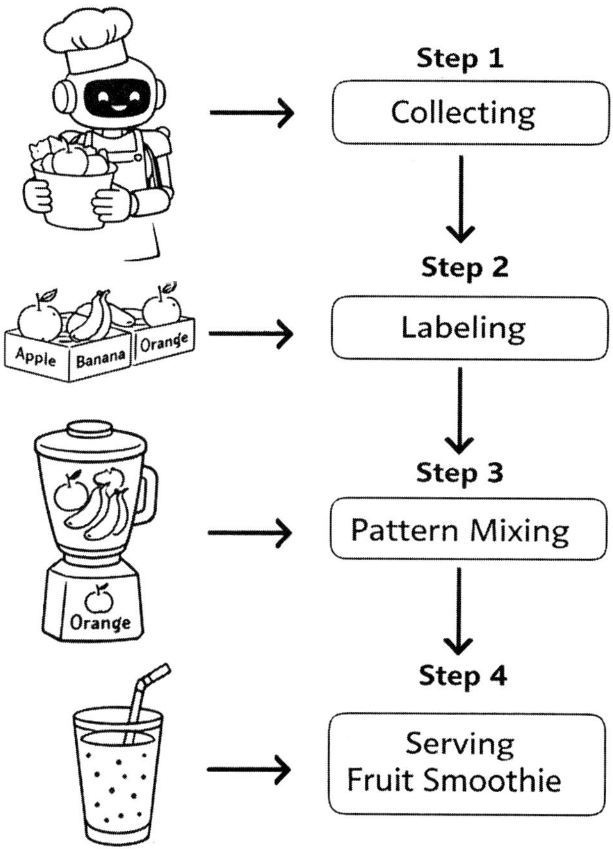

Scene Idea:

A cartoon flowchart showing a robot chef:
- **Step 1:** Collecting fruits (data)
- **Step 2:** Labeling: apple, banana, orange
- **Step 3:** Mixing patterns in a blender
- **Step 4:** Serving a fruit smoothie (prediction!)

Caption: "ML Recipe – From Data to Decisions!"

But What If the Machine Is Wrong?

Great question! Machines can make wrong predictions too.
- A spam filter might block a real email.
- A face unlock might fail in the dark.
- A shopping site might suggest something weird.

That's why ML systems must be:
- Trained with diverse data
- Updated regularly
- Tested with real-world cases

Just like you, the machine improves with feedback and correction.

Garbage In, Garbage Out

If your training data is wrong, incomplete, or biased, the machine will learn incorrectly.

This is called the "Garbage In, Garbage Out" problem in ML.

Example:
If Aryan only shows RoboCoach videos of good kicks from the right foot, it may wrongly assume that left-footed shots are always bad! That's why choosing and preparing the right data is super important.

Think & Reflect

1. Can a machine learn without examples? Why or why not?
2. Have you ever made a decision based on your past experience? How is it similar to ML?
3. Why is it important to correct mistakes in ML predictions?

Quick Game: "ML Detective"

You're building an ML model to identify types of fruit.

Here are your clues:

Fruit	Clue 1 (Color)	Clue 2 (Shape)	Clue 3 (Texture)
Apple	Red	Round	Smooth
Banana	Yellow	Curved	Smooth
Orange	Orange	Round	Bumpy

You're given a new fruit: Orange color, round, bumpy.
Can your ML detective guess the right fruit?
Yes—it's Orange. The machine compared the clues and matched the pattern.

Career Spotlight

ML Model Trainer / Data Labeling Expert

- Prepares and labels training data
- Ensures the machine sees correct examples
- Works with developers and researchers
- Important role in building ethical and accurate AI systems

Did you know? Many students work as "data annotators" part-time to help train ML tools!

Indian Example: ML in Indian Railways

Indian Railways uses ML to:

- Predict delays
- Monitor train engine health
- Improve safety and maintenance

In one case, ML helped reduce accidents by alerting engineers before parts broke down!

Abeer's Quick Tip

The first time you train a model, it will probably fail—and that's a good thing. When my early models gave wrong predictions, I realized the issue wasn't the machine—it was my data. Always check lighting, clarity, and variety of examples before retraining. Good data builds good models.

Chapter Recap

- ML starts with data—images, texts, sounds, or numbers.
- Machines learn from labeled examples to spot patterns.
- Once trained, they predict new cases.
- Tools like Teachable Machine let you try this without code!
- Clean, diverse, and unbiased data is key to good learning.
- Just like you, machines learn best with good teaching and regular feedback.

Chapter 3

Types of Machine Learning

Supervised, Unsupervised & Reinforcement (Made Easy!)

One Size Doesn't Fit All

By now, you've learned that Machine Learning (ML) helps machines learn from data and make smart decisions.

But did you know there's more than one way to teach a machine?

Just like students learn differently—some by reading, some by doing, some by asking questions—machines also learn in different styles.

Welcome to the three big families of Machine Learning:

1. Supervised Learning
2. Unsupervised Learning
3. Reinforcement Learning

Let's break these down like a fun classroom!

1. Supervised Learning – With a Teacher

What It Means:
The machine is given data along with correct answers (labels), just like a student gets examples and solutions in a math class.

Goal: Learn from known examples, then guess correctly for new ones.

Real-World Analogy:
Imagine a teacher showing you 100 pictures of animals with their names written below:

- Dog
- Cat
- Rabbit

Soon, when the teacher shows a new picture, you say, "That's a dog!"—because you learned from labeled examples.
The machine does exactly this. It's like being trained with flashcards.

Examples of Supervised ML:

- **Spam detection:** Emails are labeled "spam" or "not spam."
- **Face recognition:** Your phone learns your face by training on labeled photos.
- **Medical diagnosis:** Systems are trained on X-rays labeled "healthy" or "infected."

Beginner Tool:
Try Google's Teachable Machine
Upload photos labeled "Happy Face" and "Sad Face," and it learns to recognize your mood!

Illustration Prompt:

Visual: A robot student looking at flashcards labeled with animals and raising its hand with the correct answer when shown a new one.

2. Unsupervised Learning – No Teacher, Just Discovery

What It Means:
The machine gets data without any labels. It tries to find patterns, groups, or similarities all by itself.

Goal: Explore the data and organize it based on hidden connections.

Real-World Analogy:
Imagine entering a party where you don't know anyone. You observe people and group them in your head:
• One group likes dancing
• Another is playing video games
• Some are talking about books
You figured out groups without labels. That's what unsupervised learning does.

Examples of Unsupervised ML:
• **Customer grouping:** Shops use ML to cluster shoppers into "bargain hunters," "brand lovers," etc., without telling the system what each customer likes.

• **Social media:** Detecting similar posts or organizing photos by faces.
• **Music apps:** Creating playlists based on your listening behavior—even without labeling the genres.

Common Techniques:
• **Clustering:** Grouping similar items (like similar songs or friends)
• **Dimensionality Reduction:** Shrinking complex data (like turning a 100-question survey into 5 key patterns)

Beginner Tool:
Use Scratch + ML extension to create games where the machine learns from your drawing style and classifies it—without labels!

Illustration Prompt:

Visual: A robot in a crowd trying to group people by common traits like hat color, behavior, or speech—without anyone telling it who's who.

3. Reinforcement Learning – Learn by Trial and Error

What It Means:
The machine learns by doing—just like a gamer who improves by playing more.

It gets rewards for good actions and penalties for mistakes. Over time, it learns which actions get better results.

Goal: Maximize rewards through experience.

Real-World Analogy:
Think of training a puppy.
• If the puppy sits when you say "Sit!" → you give a treat
• If it jumps on the sofa → you say "No!"

Eventually, the puppy learns to behave. That's reinforcement learning.

Examples of Reinforcement ML:
• **Self-driving cars:** Learn to brake or steer by getting feedback from simulated drives.
• **Robots:** Learn to walk by falling and correcting themselves.
• **Game bots:** Like AlphaGo or chess engines that defeat world champions by playing millions of games.

Cool Fact:
Google's DeepMind taught a program to play Atari games better than any human—by rewarding it every time it scored!

Beginner Tool:
Try Unity ML-Agents (advanced) or watch videos of OpenAI bots learning to walk and play hide-and-seek.

Illustration Prompt:

Visual: A robot puppy learning to cross a room by avoiding obstacles and collecting coins. A scoreboard shows rewards going up.

Summary Table: Comparing ML Types

Feature	Supervised Learning	Unsupervised Learning	Reinforcement Learning
Labels Provided?	Yes	No	No (rewards instead)
Learning Style	Learn from examples	Discover hidden patterns	Trial and error
Examples	Email spam, Face unlock	Friend suggestions, Music playlists	Game bots, Robots
Goal	Predict known outputs	Group similar data	Maximize reward
Difficulty Level	Beginner-friendly	Medium	Advanced

Did You Know?

• Reinforcement Learning was inspired by behavioral psychology—the same way toddlers learn not to touch fire or spill water!
• Google Translate used unsupervised learning to figure out new languages without being told the grammar.
• Every time you skip a song on Spotify, you're reinforcing what you don't like—helping it learn your taste!

Career Spotlight

AI Trainer / Behavior Designer
These professionals help train ML models by creating real-world environments, games, or simulations.

They work on:
• Training robots to walk
• Designing smart assistants like Alexa
• Teaching drones to avoid obstacles

Skills Needed:
• Curiosity
• Logical thinking
• Experimentation
• Sometimes even game design

Think & Reflect

1. Which ML type sounds most fun to you—and why?
2. Can you think of a time you learned something through trial and error (like a game or cooking)?
3. If you were to design an ML game, what would it reward or punish?

Quick Game: Match the ML Type!

Scenario	Type of ML
Teaching a robot to classify fruit using labeled images	________
Letting a robot figure out groups of animals by shape	________
Rewarding a robot for completing a maze	________

Answers:
1. Supervised
2. Unsupervised
3. Reinforcement

Chapter Recap

• **Supervised Learning:** Learn with examples + answers (like a student with homework).
• **Unsupervised Learning:** Discover patterns without labels (like exploring a new place).
• **Reinforcement Learning:** Learn by rewards and mistakes (like playing a game).

Each type has unique strengths—and together, they power the smart world around you!

Chapter 4

ML in Daily Life

How It Works Behind the Scenes

Machine Learning Is All Around You

Did you use your phone today to unlock it with your face?
Did YouTube recommend a video you actually liked?
Did Google Maps find the fastest way to school?

If you answered "yes" to any of these, Machine Learning (ML) was your invisible helper.

We often think of ML as something futuristic, but it's already a big part of your daily life. In this chapter, we'll uncover how ML quietly powers the apps, tools, and platforms you use every day—at home, school, and even in your dreams!

Invisible but Powerful: The Hidden ML

Imagine if every time you opened an app, a tiny robot inside made decisions for you:
• "Show this video, not that one."
• "Translate this word automatically."
• "Remind her she's meeting friends at 5."
That's exactly what ML does—it runs quietly in the background, making your life easier, smoother, and smarter.
Let's dive into the many places where ML hides in plain sight!

ML on Your Phone

1. Face Unlock
Ever wondered how your phone recognizes your face?
Your camera captures your facial features (eyes, nose, jawline), then matches it with saved data. If it sees a close match—it unlocks.

ML in Action: The phone learns your face even with glasses or different lighting!

2. Auto-Correct and Predictive Text
When you type "Hppay Birtday," your phone suggests "Happy Birthday."

How does it know?
• ML learns from billions of typed messages
• It recognizes common mistakes and patterns
• It suggests based on your typing history and popular trends

ML in Action: The more you type, the smarter it gets!

3. Voice Assistants (Google Assistant, Alexa, Siri)
When you say, "What's the weather?" your voice assistant understands the words, processes them, and responds.

Behind the scenes:
• It converts voice into text (speech recognition)
• Understands your question (natural language processing)
• Finds an answer and speaks it back (text-to-speech)

ML in Action: Every voice command helps it get better at understanding YOU.

ML While You Shop

4. Product Recommendations

You search for a cricket bat. Suddenly, you see:
• Gloves
• Helmet
• Cricket shoes
• A cricket coaching ad!

ML learns your interest from search history and suggests what you might like.

ML in Action: Makes shopping feel magical—and addictive!

5. Fraud Detection in Payments

Have you ever received a message like "Suspicious login attempt"?

Banks and wallets use ML to detect unusual behavior:
• Logging in from a new location
• Sudden big transaction
• Buying strange items

ML in Action: Stops fraud before it happens.

ML in Entertainment & Gaming

6. Netflix & YouTube Suggestions

Why does YouTube always know what you want to watch next?

ML tracks:

- What you've watched
- What you skipped
- What similar users liked
- Time of day, location, device

It uses all this to recommend content.

ML in Action: Keeps you watching longer (sometimes too long!).

7. Game Difficulty Adjustment

In some video games, enemies become harder or easier based on your skill.
That's ML learning how well you play—and adjusting the challenge.

Example: Racing games adjust car speed to match your level.
ML bots in chess or PUBG learn to play smarter with time.

ML in Action: Makes your game fun, not frustrating.

ML in Education

8. Personalized Learning Apps

Apps like BYJU'S, Khan Academy, and Doubtnut use ML to:

- Track what questions you get wrong
- Suggest easier or related videos
- Give tests based on your progress

It's like having a digital tutor who understands your strengths and weaknesses.

ML in Action: Learns how you learn!

9. Language Translation

Ever used Google Translate?
You type: "How are you?" → Get "कैसे हो?"

ML models are trained on millions of bilingual texts and learn how languages work.

Newer tools can even translate speech in real time!

ML in Action: Breaking language barriers globally.

ML in Transport & Navigation

10. Google Maps & Ola/Uber
You open Google Maps to find the fastest route.

It uses ML to:
• Predict traffic patterns
• Suggest alternate roads
• Estimate arrival time (ETA)

Apps like Uber use ML to match drivers with passengers and predict fares.

ML in Action: Saves time, reduces fuel, and avoids traffic jams.
11. Self-Driving Cars

Though not common in India yet, self-driving cars use reinforcement learning to:
• Detect lanes
• Recognize pedestrians
• Make safe driving decisions

Companies like Tesla, Waymo, and BMW are training ML models with real road data.

ML in Health & Safety

12. Fitness Trackers & Smartwatches
Your watch says, "Time to stand!" or "You slept for 6 hrs 38 mins."

ML tracks:
• Your movement
• Sleep patterns
• Heart rate
• Step count
It compares your data with healthy trends and gives advice.

ML in Action: Helps build healthy habits.

13. COVID-19 Detection

ML helped scientists:
• Detect COVID in X-rays
• Predict case surges
• Track contact tracing via apps like Aarogya Setu
Even vaccine development used ML models to study protein structures!

Hidden ML at School

14. Plagiarism Checkers
Teachers use tools like Turnitin or QuillBot to detect copied content.

These tools:
• Read and compare your text to billions of documents
• Detect patterns, tone, and originality

ML in Action: Keeps your homework honest!

15. Attendance Monitoring with Face Recognition
Some schools and offices now use cameras to auto-mark attendance by recognizing faces.

No punching cards or registers—just look and log in.

Illustration Prompt

Scene Idea: A child in their room using a phone, tablet, and smart speaker, with hidden cartoon-style ML robots working inside each device—one suggesting music, another fixing typos, one showing maps.

Caption: "Meet Your Hidden Helpers – ML in Action!"

Think & Reflect

1. How many ML tools did you unknowingly use today?
2. Which ML-powered app do you find most helpful—and why?
3. If you could build your own ML-powered app, what would it do?

Try It Yourself!

"ML Detectives" Activity

For 24 hours, track every time you:
• Get a suggestion
• See an ad
• Get a message or correction
• Use maps, voice, or face unlock
Log them in a journal and write "What ML did here?"
You'll be surprised how often it appears!

Career Spotlight

AI Product Designer

Designs smart apps for education, shopping, games, or health.

They decide:
• What features the app should have
• How ML will improve the experience
• What data the app should learn from

Skills:
• Creativity
• Tech understanding
• UI/UX design

Many Indian startups now hire teenagers as junior design interns!

India Shining: ML in Our Everyday Bharat

• **Kisan e-Mitra:** Uses ML to suggest fertilizer and crop plans to farmers.
• **Aadhaar:** Uses biometric ML for identity verification.

- **E-RUPI & UPI:** Predict fraud and ensure secure payments.

India is using ML not just for luxury—but for inclusion and access.

Chapter Recap

- ML is quietly working behind your favorite apps and tools.
- It personalizes shopping, learning, entertainment, health, and travel.
- You use ML multiple times a day—without even realizing it!
- India is using ML to empower farmers, teachers, doctors, and YOU.

Chapter 5

Cool ML Projects You Can Try! (Games, Voice, Art & More)

Ready to Build with Machine Learning?

By now, you've learned what Machine Learning is, how it works, and where it shows up in your everyday life. But here comes the most exciting part:

YOU can build your own Machine Learning projects—right now.
No fancy laptop, no programming degree, and no waiting till college.
Just your curiosity, a little creativity, and an internet connection.

In this chapter, we'll show you simple, fun, and hands-on ML projects that you can try as a beginner. Whether you love games, music, drawing, or solving real-life problems, there's a project for you!

Let's unlock your inner ML creator.

Project 1: Make a Rock–Paper–Scissors Game That Learns!

What It Teaches:

- Image classification
- Pattern recognition
- Game development basics

Tools:

- Google Teachable Machine
- Scratch or MIT App Inventor

Steps:

1. Go to teachablemachine.withgoogle.com
2. Select "Image Project" → "Standard"
3. Create 3 classes: "Rock," "Paper," "Scissors"
4. Use your webcam to record yourself showing hand gestures for each class
5. Train the model
6. Export it and connect to a Scratch game where your computer plays against you!

Result:

A fun game where your webcam reads your move and plays back—like a robot friend!

From My Experience

The first time I trained a Rock–Paper–Scissors model, it confused "Rock" and "Paper" because my hand positions were inconsistent. I had to retrain it with clearer examples. That trial-and-error process actually helped me understand reinforcement and pattern learning better.

Illustration Prompt:

Scene of a kid showing “rock” with their hand, a laptop recognizing the gesture and displaying “Paper! I win!”

Caption: “When your computer becomes your gaming buddy!”

Project 2: Create a Voice-Controlled Assistant

What It Teaches:

- Voice command recognition
- Action automation
- Speech-to-text ML

Tools:

- Teachable Machine (Audio project)
- MIT App Inventor
- Your voice!

Steps:

1. Open Teachable Machine → Select “Audio”

2. Record your voice saying "Play," "Pause," "Stop" or any custom words
3. Train and export your model
4. Use MIT App Inventor to build a simple mobile app that responds to voice commands

Result:
A mini Alexa that follows your voice for small tasks like playing a song or showing a picture!

Illustration Prompt:

A girl speaking to her phone: "Play music," with a speaker icon lighting up and a robot DJ dancing on screen.

Project 3: Make ML-Powered Art!

What It Teaches:
- Generative AI
- Visual creativity
- Neural networks

Tools:

- DALL·E 2 (by OpenAI)
- QuickDraw (by Google)
- DeepDream Generator

Steps:

1. Try QuickDraw—the ML model guesses your doodles in under 20 seconds!
2. Go to openai.com/dall-e
3. Type any wild idea like: "A cat riding a rocket in Van Gogh style"
4. DALL·E generates AI artwork instantly!
5. Try remixing your art with DeepDream or Canva

Result:

Unique, AI-generated art pieces you can print, share, or use in school projects!

Project 4: Build Your Own Emoji Predictor

What It Teaches:

- Natural language processing (NLP)
- Text classification

Tools:

- MLforKids.io
- Scratch Extension for ML

Steps:

1. Visit mlforkids.io
2. Train your model by entering phrases and matching them with emojis:
    - o "Yay, I won!" →
    - o "I'm tired." →
    - o "This is scary." →
3. Add more data and train
4. Connect to Scratch to create a chatbot that shows emojis based on

what you type

Result:
A chatbot that understands your emotion and responds with the right emoji!

Project 5: AI Science Fair Idea – Plant Health Detector

What It Teaches:
• Image classification
• Real-life problem-solving
• ML for sustainability

Tools:
• Teachable Machine
• Smartphone + ML camera app

Steps:
1. Take 50–100 pictures of healthy and unhealthy plants
2. Label and train them in Teachable Machine
3. Use a camera-based app to scan real plants
4. Your model will say "Healthy" or "Needs Water" or "Infected"

Result:
An AI-powered gardening tool to detect plant health and suggest care!

Indian Use Case Inspiration

Farmers in Andhra Pradesh are using similar ML apps to detect crop diseases using images and receive instant tips in Telugu and Hindi!

Think & Reflect

1. Which project sounds most exciting to you—and why?

2. What real-life problem would you like to solve with ML?
3. Can art and creativity mix with technology? How?

Bonus Project Ideas

Project Idea	What You'll Learn
Hand-gesture robot controller	Image recognition + robotics
ML poetry generator	Natural language generation
Mood-based music player	Emotion detection + ML playlist
ML quiz bot for your class	Classification + quiz logic
ML food suggestion app	Text prediction + recipe finder

Helpful Beginner Tools & Platforms

Tool / Website	What It Does
Teachable Machine	Image/voice/pose classification
Scratch + ML Extension	Build games with ML models
MIT App Inventor	Create ML-powered mobile apps
MLforKids.io	Easy drag-and-drop NLP and classifiers
QuickDraw	Google's sketch recognition ML demo
DALL·E / DeepDream	AI-based image generation from text
Canva with AI tools	Design posters using smart tools

Activity: Create a "ML Project Planner" Page

Make a chart with:

- Project Name
- What it will do
- Tool you'll use
- Data you'll need

• What you'll learn
Hang it near your study desk to stay inspired!

Career Spotlight

Creative Technologist
Combines art + coding + ML to create music videos, digital installations, games, and interactive apps.

Famous Examples:
• Google's creative lab engineers
• AR filters creators on Instagram/Snapchat
• Indian AI artists experimenting with heritage and dance

Skills:
• Design thinking
• Beginner coding
• Interest in human + machine interaction

Abeer's Quick Tip

Start small. Don't try to build a complex ML app on day one. Train a two-category model first (like "Smile" vs. "Serious"). Once that works confidently, expand. Machine Learning rewards patience more than speed.

Chapter Recap

• You can start building ML projects with free tools—no coding required!
• Projects include games, art, gardening tools, and emotion bots
• Platforms like Teachable Machine, MLforKids, and Scratch make learning fun
• Creativity + curiosity = amazing ML possibilities

Chapter 6

ML in the Real World

Healthcare, Farming, Banking & Education

When ML Goes Big: Real-Life Superpowers

We've seen how Machine Learning (ML) is in our phones, games, and even emojis. But now it's time to go beyond screens.
Let's step into the real world—where ML is not just entertaining or helpful, but life-changing. From saving lives in hospitals to boosting crop yields on Indian farms, ML is transforming every corner of society.

In this chapter, we'll explore how ML is used in 4 big sectors:

1. Healthcare
2. Agriculture
3. Banking & Finance
4. Education

Let's uncover how ML is making the world smarter, safer, and more inclusive.

1. ML in Healthcare – Saving Lives with Smarter Tech

Imagine if a computer could scan your X-ray and say, "This looks like pneumonia," or help doctors predict a heart attack before it happens. That's not science fiction anymore—it's happening with ML in medicine.

How ML Helps:

• Analyzing thousands of medical images (like CT scans and MRIs)
• Detecting diseases like cancer, COVID-19, or eye damage in diabetes
• Monitoring patients in ICUs
• Predicting health risks based on data (like past checkups, vitals, and genetics)

Example:

• Aravind Eye Hospital, India: Uses ML to detect diabetic retinopathy (an eye disease) early by scanning retina images.
• COVID-19 X-ray Screening: ML tools were trained on chest X-rays to identify early signs of COVID with high accuracy.

Tools Used:

• TensorFlow for medical imaging
• IBM Watson for oncology
• ML algorithms for remote diagnostics in rural clinics

Illustration Prompt:

A doctor and a robot looking at a scan of lungs on a screen. The robot highlights a spot and says: "Early infection detected."

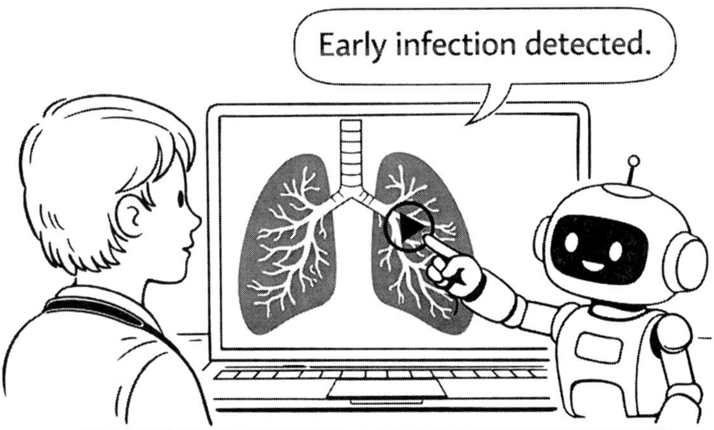

When your computer becomes your gaming buddy!

Think & Reflect

- Would you feel safe being treated with help from an AI doctor?
- What are the benefits and risks of using machines in hospitals?

2. ML in Agriculture – Helping Farmers Grow Smarter

India is an agricultural country. Millions of farmers depend on rain, soil, and timing.

But what if a smartphone could help a farmer decide:

- When to sow?
- Which fertilizer to use?
- Whether crops are infected?

That's the promise of ML in agriculture.

How ML Helps:

- Analyzing satellite images for crop health
- Predicting rainfall and climate patterns
- Identifying pests or diseases from leaf photos

• Recommending the right amount of fertilizer or water

Example:

• Plantix App: Farmers upload a photo of a leaf, and ML tells them what disease it has and how to fix it.
• Kisan AI by Wadhwani Institute: Uses AI for soil reports and irrigation suggestions in local languages.
• e-Choupal: An initiative where ML models predict market prices for crops to reduce farmer exploitation.

Benefits:

• Increases yield
• Reduces waste
• Empowers small farmers with smart tools

Illustration Prompt:

An Indian farmer taking a photo of his crops. A cartoon ML cloud above shows sun, rain, disease warning, and price predictions.

Try This:

Imagine you're designing an ML app for farmers in your village. What features will you add? Will it support Hindi or your local language?

3. ML in Banking & Finance – Smarter Money, Safer Systems

Money moves fast—and fraudsters move faster! ML helps banks keep your money safe while making your experience smoother.

How ML Helps:
- Detecting fraud in real time (suspicious transactions)
- Approving or denying loans based on financial behavior
- Predicting credit risk
- Recommending personalized offers, savings plans, or credit cards

Example:
- HDFC Bank uses ML to offer the right product to the right customer.
- RBI's "Mani App" uses ML to help visually impaired users identify currency notes.
- UPI Systems use ML to block scams and secure payments.

Fraud Detection:
ML models watch for:
- Strange login times
- Too many failed passwords
- Spending spikes

They alert banks instantly—much faster than a human could.

Did You Know?

India's Unified Payments Interface (UPI) uses ML to process over 10 billion transactions monthly—detecting fraud, verifying users, and predicting user intent!

Illustration Prompt:

A child using a digital wallet while a smart ML guardian in the background watches for scam attempts and blocks danger signals.

Think & Reflect

• Have you ever received a message warning about suspicious bank activity?
• Can ML be fair when approving loans? What happens if the model is biased?

4. ML in Education – Learning Gets Personal

Every student learns differently. Some love math, some struggle with English. ML helps teachers personalize lessons so that every student gets what they need—when they need it.

How ML Helps:
• Tracking student performance
• Suggesting custom exercises or videos
• Predicting where a student might struggle

• Automating feedback and grading

Example:
• BYJU'S & Khan Academy: Use ML to offer "next best lesson" suggestions based on test results.
• Google Classroom: Recommends study materials and grades short answers.
• CBSE AI Curriculum: Introduces students to ML through simple projects.

Teacher Assistant:
ML can grade MCQs, spot copied text, and even detect patterns in student engagement.

Indian Government Initiatives:

• AI for Youth Program (CBSE + Intel): Free ML training for school students
• Diksha App: Personalized learning for teachers and students using ML-based content curation
• NITI Aayog's ATL Labs: Encourages students to create ML-powered solutions for real-world problems

Try This:

Design a chatbot that helps students revise before exams. What questions will it ask? What ML features would make it smarter?

Career Spotlight

Agri-Tech Innovator
Builds ML tools for farmers—apps, drones, sensors, and more.

Skills:
• Agriculture knowledge

• Data science basics
• Design thinking
• Language localization

Chapter Recap

• ML is changing how we heal, grow food, handle money, and learn.
• In healthcare, it diagnoses diseases and tracks patients.
• In farming, it predicts weather, identifies diseases, and increases yields.
• In banking, it stops fraud and improves user experience.
• In education, it personalizes learning and supports teachers.

ML is not just a tech tool—it's a social transformer.

Chapter 7

How to Start Learning ML Today (No Coding Needed!)

You Don't Need to Be a Genius or a Coder

"Do I need to know Python?"
"Should I wait until college?"
"I'm only 13, can I still learn Machine Learning?"

The answer to all these questions is YES—you can start right now. In fact, many school students across India and the world are already building smart ML apps, games, chatbots, and projects—all without writing a single line of code!

This chapter will guide you step by step through how to start your ML journey today, using beginner-friendly platforms, daily habits, and free tools.
Let's get you learning like a machine… but with a human heart.

Open the First Door: Curiosity

Before you touch a keyboard, you need the most important tool—curiosity.

Ask yourself:
• Why does my phone unlock with my face?
• How does Netflix know what I want?
• Can I train a machine to understand my drawings?

If you're asking questions like these—you're already on the ML path.

Tool #1: Google Teachable Machine (No Code)

Website: https://teachablemachine.withgoogle.com

What It Does:

Lets you train a computer to recognize:
• **Images** (e.g., different hand gestures or facial expressions)
• **Sounds** (e.g., clap, snap, voice commands)
• **Poses** (e.g., yoga poses, dancing moves)

Why It's Great:
• Free and works in browser
• Kid-friendly interface
• Works with webcam/microphone
• Instant feedback and testing

Your First Activity:

Train it to recognize:
• You smiling vs. frowning
• Clap vs. snap
• "Hello" vs. "Bye" voice

Try changing your lighting or camera angle and see how well it still works!

Tool #2: ML for Kids

Website: https://machinelearningforkids.co.uk

What It Does:
• Combines ML training with Scratch, a block-based coding platform
• Lets you train models with your own data (like emojis, moods, or questions)
• Helps you create ML-powered games or chatbots

Project Ideas:
• An emoji suggestion chatbot
• A quiz app that guesses your mood
• A classifier that tells whether your message is positive or negative

Tool #3: Quick, Creative, and Visual Platforms

1. QuickDraw (Google AI Experiments)
• Website: https://quickdraw.withgoogle.com
• Draw doodles in 20 seconds, and ML guesses what you're making!

2. DALL·E (by OpenAI)
• Website: https://openai.com/dall-e
• Type something creative like:
"An elephant doing yoga in the mountains"—and DALL·E draws it using ML!

3. AutoDraw (Google)
• Website: https://autodraw.com
• You draw a rough shape, and ML guesses what you're trying to draw and corrects it into a clean image.

Perfect for young artists and design lovers!

Tool #4: Scratch + ML Extension

- Combine Scratch (block coding) with pre-trained ML models
- **Make games that respond to:**
    - o Camera gestures
    - o Sounds
    - o Typed input

Example Game:

- **"Angry Alien":** The character jumps when you frown and ducks when you smile!

Tool #5: MIT App Inventor

- Create mobile apps with drag-and-drop blocks
- **Add ML extensions to:**
    - o Respond to speech
    - o Recognize gestures
    - o Classify objects

Project Idea:

- Build a mobile assistant that responds to your "Good Morning!" and shows you the weather.

Government Programs to Explore

AI For Youth (CBSE + Intel)

- Free beginner AI and ML curriculum
- Project-based learning
- Available for Grades 8–12
- Schools can register with CBSE or local AI labs

Atal Innovation Mission (AIM)

• Part of NITI Aayog
• Promotes innovation and ML learning through ATL Labs in schools
• Students build prototypes for social problems using smart tech

Daily Habits to Build ML Skills (Without Screens)

1. Ask Questions

o Why did Google show me this ad?
o What could happen if ML made a mistake?

2. Sketch Ideas

o Draw your dream ML app
o Map the steps it might need (data, learning, decision)

3. Read Simple Blogs or Watch Videos

o Start with YouTube channels like Simplilearn Kids, Code.org, or CBSE AI playlist

4. Observe Patterns

o In your behavior, apps, weather, and games

Fun Exercises

Game: "ML or Not?"

Say "ML" or "Not ML" for each situation:

1. Your microwave heats for 1 minute → __________
2. Instagram suggests a reel you'll love → __________
3. School bell rings at 9 AM → ____________
4. YouTube plays similar music → ___________

Answers:

1. Not ML
2. ML

3. Not ML
4. ML

Think & Reflect

• What did you learn today without a teacher's help?
• How can a machine do something similar?
• What's one topic you'd love to teach an ML model?

Career Spotlight

ML Enthusiast → ML Explorer → ML Maker

Even before becoming a Data Scientist, there are cool junior roles like:

• Student Innovator (Atal Labs)
• School ML Club Leader
• Intern at AI startups (many allow age 15+ with parental consent!)

Explore online certificates from platforms like:

• Google AI
• Code.org
• IBM AI Education for Youth

Chapter Recap

• You don't need coding to start ML. Just curiosity and a few tools!
• Platforms like Teachable Machine, ML for Kids, and QuickDraw are free and fun
• India's youth programs make ML learning easy and inclusive
• Daily habits like asking questions, observing patterns, and playing with tools can grow your ML muscle

Chapter 8

ML vs. AI

What's the Difference?

Aren't AI and ML the Same Thing?

You've heard both words often:

• AI (Artificial Intelligence)
• ML (Machine Learning)

They're sometimes used like twins. But here's the truth: ML is a part of AI, just like algebra is a part of mathematics.

In this chapter, we'll explore:

• What is Artificial Intelligence?
• What is Machine Learning?
• How are they different?
• How are they connected?

And we'll make it fun, clear, and super easy to remember.

What Is Artificial Intelligence (AI)?

Artificial Intelligence is when machines are designed to act smart—like humans.

These machines can:

- Understand language
- Recognize images
- Make decisions
- Play games
- Move and sense the world (like robots!)

Key Idea:

AI is not just about learning, it's about thinking and behaving intelligently.

AI covers:

- Rule-based systems
- Robotics
- Computer vision
- Natural language processing
- And yes… Machine Learning

Real-Life Examples of AI:

AI Use Case	What It Does
Google Translate	Translates your words using smart rules
Chess App	Makes moves to beat you
Alexa/Siri	Talks like a person, answers questions
Face ID	Identifies your face to unlock phone
ChatGPT	Writes poems, stories, and essays

What Is Machine Learning (ML)?

Machine Learning is a method used inside AI that teaches machines to learn from data—without being programmed every time.

ML doesn't follow fixed rules. It learns patterns from examples and makes predictions.

Examples of ML:

ML Use Case	What It Does
YouTube recommendations	Suggests videos based on your behavior
Spam detection	Filters out bad emails based on past ones
Teachable Machine	Learns to recognize your gestures or voice
Instagram filters	Predicts faces, applies effects

The Relationship Between AI and ML

Let's draw a picture in your mind:

mathematica

CopyEdit

Artificial Intelligence (Big Circle)
├── Machine Learning (Smaller Circle inside AI)
    ├── Deep Learning (Even Smaller Circle inside ML)

So:

- All Machine Learning is AI,
- But not all AI is Machine Learning.

Some AI uses rules written by humans.
Some AI uses ML, which learns from data.

Illustration Prompt

Draw a Russian nesting doll:
• The big doll = AI
• The middle doll = ML
• The tiny doll = Deep Learning

Caption: "AI is the big idea. ML is the brainy middle. Deep Learning is the expert child!"

Rule-Based AI vs. Learning AI

Rule-Based AI (Old School AI):
• Follows "IF–THEN" rules
• **Example:**
IF the user types "hello" → THEN say "Hi! How can I help?"

Great for simple tasks, but breaks if things change.

Learning AI (Modern AI with ML):
• Learns from examples and data
• **Example:**
Feed it 10,000 "hello" messages in different languages—it learns patterns and says "Hi!" in many ways.

Analogy:
• Rule-based AI = A calculator (always follows fixed steps)
• ML-based AI = A student (learns from practice and improves)

What Is Deep Learning?

It's a special type of Machine Learning that uses neural networks (inspired by the human brain). These models learn very complex patterns.

Used in:

- Self-driving cars
- ChatGPT
- DALL·E (AI art tools)
- Google Lens (image recognition)

But don't worry—you'll learn more about Deep Learning in higher classes!

Let's Play: AI or ML?

Say whether each one uses AI (rules) or ML (learns from data)

Scenario	AI or ML?
A game character that says "Well played!" after every win	AI (rule)
A robot that learns to walk by trial and error	ML
A website that shows products based on your past views	ML
A chatbot that answers "Hello" to every greeting	AI (rule)

Career Spotlight

AI/ML Researcher

- Builds smart systems that think and learn
- Explores ethics, safety, and future of AI
- Works on AI models in speech, vision, robotics

Skills:

- Math & logic
- Python or R
- Data analysis
- Curious, creative thinking

Many start with free online courses on AI basics before doing degrees in Computer Science or Data Science.

Think & Reflect

- What are 3 smart things a human can do that machines still can't?
- Can ML make mistakes? Why?
- Should all decisions (like medical or legal) be made by AI?

Chapter Recap

Term	Meaning
AI	The big idea: machines that think and act smart
ML	A method within AI that learns from data
Deep Learning	A type of ML inspired by the human brain
Rule-Based AI	Follows fixed instructions
Learning AI	Improves by analyzing examples

AI is the dream.
ML is the machine that's learning how to dream.

Chapter 9

Ethics in Machine Learning

Bias, Fairness & Responsibility

Just Because We Can... Should We?

Machine Learning is powerful. It can help doctors, students, farmers—even build self-driving cars! But with great power comes a big question:

Is the machine being fair, safe, and kind?

That's where ethics comes in.

In this chapter, you'll learn how Machine Learning can sometimes go wrong—and what we must do to make it right. Let's talk about bias, fairness, safety, privacy, and responsibility in ML.

What Are ML Ethics?

Ethics in ML means making sure that the machine:

- Treats everyone fairly
- Protects people's rights and data
- Does not harm or mislead
- Acts transparently and responsibly

Bias in ML – When Machines Are Not Fair

Imagine teaching a robot to recognize faces—but you only give it photos of boys.
When it sees a girl's face, it says, "I don't know what this is."

That's bias—when a system works well for some people but not for others.

How Bias Happens:

- **Bad data:** If the training data is not diverse.
- **Human mistakes:** If we add our own unfair assumptions.
- **Skewed labels**: If certain groups are labeled incorrectly.

Real-Life Examples:

- A job app rejected women's resumes because it learned from past hiring data (which favored men).
- A face recognition system struggled to identify darker skin tones.
- A language model predicted negative words when given names from minority communities.

Why Bias Is Dangerous

- It can cause unfair decisions (e.g., denying loans, jobs, or school admissions).
- It can hurt feelings or even cause harm.
- It spreads inequality instead of solving it.

Illustration Prompt

Scene of two children (a boy and a girl) trying to enter a digital door. The ML system greets the boy but ignores the girl. A red warning says "Biased Training Detected."

Caption: "A smart machine isn't always a fair one—until we train it right."

Privacy Matters – Your Data, Your Rights

ML systems often use your personal data: photos, voice, messages, or health info.

That means:
- You have the right to know what's being collected
- You can choose to share or not share
- Companies must protect your data

Golden Rule:
"Just because you can collect data, doesn't mean you should."

Can Machines Be Kind?

No, machines don't have feelings. But they can be programmed to act ethically:
- Don't discriminate
- Ask for permission before using data
- Explain why they made a decision

This is called "Responsible AI" or "Ethical ML"

AI for Good – Using ML to Help, Not Harm

Good Examples:
- ML apps that detect fake news

- Models that remove bias from old systems
- Chatbots that help report bullying or abuse
- Tools that make education accessible in local languages

India's own AI for All mission promotes building AI that helps:
- Farmers
- Students
- Doctors
- The Environment

Building Fair & Inclusive ML – 5 Simple Principles

Principle	What It Means
1. Fairness	No group is left out or treated badly
2. Accountability	Humans stay in control and take responsibility
3. Transparency	Machines must explain how they decide
4. Safety	No harm should be caused
5. Privacy	People's data must be protected

Let's Make a "Responsible ML Pledge"

As a future ML builder, I promise to:
- Use fair and diverse data
- Ask "Is this helpful or harmful?"
- Explain my model's goal and output
- Respect privacy and consent
- Fix and learn from mistakes

Activity: "Spot the Bias" Game

Here are some examples. Can you find the ethical issue in each?

Scenario	What's Wrong?
A job app shows only male candidates	____________
A game recognizes only light-skinned players	____________
A study app uses student data without asking	____________
A chatbot uses mean words to joke	____________

Answers:

1. Gender bias
2. Racial bias
3. Privacy issue
4. Harmful behavior

Career Spotlight

AI Ethics Researcher / Policy Expert

- Studies the impact of ML systems on society
- Helps companies write rules for fairness and safety
- Works with governments, schools, and startups

Skills:

- Critical thinking
- Law + technology
- Communication
- Ethics training (some NGOs even have student internships!)

Think & Reflect

- Should machines be allowed to make life-changing decisions?
- How can we make ML more inclusive for all?
- What should happen if an ML system causes harm?

Abeer's Quick Tip

Before building any ML project, ask yourself one question: "Who could this accidentally harm?" Even simple school projects should be tested for fairness. Responsible ML begins with awareness, not advanced coding.

Chapter Recap

- ML must be fair, safe, and kind—not just smart.
- Bias happens when training data is not diverse or correct.
- We must protect privacy and ask before collecting personal data.
- Good ML helps everyone; bad ML can cause harm.
- YOU can be a responsible ML creator by following 5 ethical principles.

"Build not just intelligent machines—but wise ones."

Chapter 10

Women & Youth in ML

Join the Movement!

A New Generation of ML Trailblazers

You've seen how Machine Learning can change lives and solve big problems. But who are the people building these smart systems?

Here's something amazing:
Young people—and especially girls—are changing the face of AI and ML.

This chapter is your invitation to be part of the movement. Whether you dream of creating an app to help farmers, making AI art, or fixing digital inequality—you belong in ML.

Let's explore how young minds and bold hearts are shaping the future of Machine Learning.

Where Are the Girls in ML?

Sadly, women and girls have been underrepresented in science and tech fields for many years. But that's changing fast—thanks to support, awareness, and powerful stories.

The Problem:
- Fewer girls are encouraged to take coding in school
- Not enough role models are shown in books or media
- Many think "tech is not for me"

The Change:
- Girls across India are leading AI projects
- More schools have STEM clubs for girls
- Government and companies are running coding camps for underrepresented youth

"You can't be what you can't see—so let's meet the changemakers!"

Real Stories of Women in ML

1. Dr. Fei-Fei Li (USA / China)
- Co-director of Stanford's AI Lab
- Created ImageNet, a huge ML database
- Advocates for "Human-Centered AI"

Quote: *"AI is not just about tech—it's about people."*

2. Joy Buolamwini (Ghana / USA)
- Founder of the Algorithmic Justice League
- Spoke out about facial recognition bias
- Created films and poems on AI fairness

Quote: *"The coded gaze is not neutral."*

3. Dr. Timnit Gebru (Eritrea / Ethiopia)
• Worked at Google AI
• Researches ethics, fairness, and discrimination in ML
• Helps women and Black youth enter tech fields

Quote: *"Who gets to define what 'intelligent' means?"*

Indian Girls Leading in ML

Ananya Grover (Delhi, India)
• Teen who created "Maitri," an ML-powered app to support elderly people during COVID-19
• Finalist in international coding contests

Ritika Pandey (Lucknow, India)
• Built a soil-testing ML tool to help small farmers
• Trained under CBSE's AI for Youth programme
• Wants to work on climate tech!

Aisha Naaz (Bihar, India)
• Developed a chatbot to help girls talk about menstrual health
• Created using Scratch + MLforKids
• Won local science fair and was invited to ATL Summit

Global Youth Making ML Waves

• A 14-year-old from Japan made an ML app to detect plastic in rivers
• A Kenyan teen built a voice assistant in Swahili
• Girls from the Philippines built a tool to fight online bullying using text classification

All of them started with free tools, questions, and courage.

Programs You Can Join

Program	Who It's For	What It Offers
CBSE AI For Youth	Indian students (Grades 8–12)	ML training + project showcase
Girls Who Code (India/USA)	Girls aged 12–18	Coding + mentorship
Atal Innovation Mission	All school students	ML project support + ATL Labs
She Codes (India)	Girls from small towns	Workshops + boot-camps

These programs are open to all genders and encourage inclusivity!

Your First Steps to Join

1. Find a local coding club or form one with friends
2. Use Teachable Machine or MLforKids to build a small project
3. Present it in your school science fair or ATL showcase
4. Follow ML leaders on YouTube, Instagram, or LinkedIn
5. Share your journey—every voice matters!

Activity: Design Your ML Hero Poster

Choose one inspiring woman or youth in ML and design a poster:

- Their photo or sketch
- What they built
- What challenge they solved
- Your favorite quote from them

Stick it in your room or school computer lab to inspire others!

Illustration Prompt

A diverse group of children (girls and boys) from different Indian states, working together on laptops and whiteboards. One is showing an ML project to a teacher. Flags, code snippets, and "AI For Good" posters in the background.

Myth Busters

Myth	Truth
"ML is only for geniuses."	ML is for curious learners like you!
"Girls aren't good at tech."	Girls across India are winning AI awards!
"You need to be rich to learn ML."	Most tools are free and online!

Think & Reflect

- Do you see someone like you in the ML field? Why or why not?
- If you had to solve a problem in your home or community using ML, what would it be?
- Who would you teach ML to—and why?

Career Spotlight

Youth AI Innovator
Many ML leaders start before age 18!

You could be a:

- Science fair winner
- App creator
- School workshop mentor
- ATL Summit speaker

Tip: Your project doesn't have to be "perfect." It just has to solve a real problem with heart.

Chapter Recap

- Girls and youth are transforming Machine Learning—and so can you.
- From chatbots to climate apps, teens are solving real problems.
- Programs like AI For Youth and ATL support students with tools, mentors, and platforms.
- Representation matters. Every new ML creator inspires someone else.
- ML is not just for some—it's for everyone.

"You don't have to wait to grow up to change the world. With ML, you can start today."

Chapter 11

Careers in Machine Learning

What Can You Become?

From Curious Student to ML Superstar

You've now explored what Machine Learning is, how it works, and how young people across India and the world are building ML-powered solutions.

Now let's ask the big question:

Can you build a career in Machine Learning?
Yes, you absolutely can. And this chapter will show you how!

Whether you want to be a coder, artist, teacher, entrepreneur, or doctor—ML has a space for you. Let's explore the exciting world of ML careers, step by step.

Why ML Careers Matter (And Are Growing!)

• India is expected to have over 1 million jobs in AI and ML by 2030
• ML is used in education, environment, banking, healthcare, art, defense, law, journalism, agriculture, and space
• Companies need ethical, curious, young minds to build the future

ML is not just a job—it's a toolbox for every career.

Top ML Career Paths

Here's a look at 10 amazing careers where ML is the core skill:

Role	What They Do
1. ML Engineer	Builds and trains ML models for apps and systems
2. Data Scientist	Understands patterns in data and predicts outcomes
3. AI Product Manager	Plans and manages ML-powered products
4. NLP Specialist	Works with speech, language, and chatbots
5. Computer Vision Engineer	Builds models that recognize images and video
6. Robotics Engineer	Combines ML with movement and sensors
7. AI Ethics Specialist	Ensures fairness, privacy, and safety in ML
8. ML Educator / Trainer	Teaches others how to use ML tools
9. ML for Social Good Researcher	Uses ML to solve environmental, health, or social issues

10. AI Artist / Creative Technologist	Combines ML with music, drawing, film, or storytelling

What Should You Study?

Start Early With:

- Mathematics (especially patterns, logic, and statistics)
- Science projects using data
- Computer basics and logic puzzles
- Apps like Scratch, Blockly, or Python on Code.org

After Class 10:

Stream	Subjects
Science	Math, Physics, Computer Science, English
Commerce + AI	Math, Business, Computer Applications
Humanities + AI	Logic, Language, Psychology, Informatics

Courses After Class 12:

- B.Tech in Computer Science / AI / Data Science
- B.Sc in Data Analytics
- BCA with AI modules
- Integrated B.Sc + M.Sc (Maths + AI focus)
- Design + AI for creative tech careers

Many Indian universities like IITs, IIIT-Hyderabad, Ashoka University, Amity University, and SRM have launched ML/AI-focused degrees.

Short-Term Learning Paths (Great for Teens!)

Platform	What You Can Learn
Google AI	Beginner AI and ML courses
Coursera	Free ML basics from Stanford, IITs

YouTube Channels	"Simplilearn," "Codebasics," "Tech with Tim"
CBSE AI Curriculum	School modules, ATL kits, and competitions
Intel AI For Youth	Project-based certification programs
Kaggle (Beginner Mode)	Hands-on ML challenges for students

Many of these offer free certificates—great for your portfolio!

Real-World Indian ML Career Stories

Tanvi, 17 – Bengaluru
Built an ML app that analyzes traffic patterns and gives alerts to drivers. Presented at the CBSE ATL National Showcase.

Aarav, 15 – Nagpur
Used ML for identifying fake news articles using Teachable Machine and shared it in school media club.

Fatima, 16 – Kolkata
Started as an MLforKids user, now building her own fashion recommendation bot. Wants to mix tech with fashion!

Where Do ML Experts Work?

Sector	Example Roles
Healthcare	Predict disease, scan X-rays
Agriculture	Monitor crops, predict rainfall
E-commerce	Build recommendation engines
Startups	Build AI-powered apps
EdTech	Smart learning platforms
Art & Culture	AI art, film, design

Space & Defense	Navigation systems, surveillance tools

Big Indian employers:

• TCS, Infosys, Wipro, HCL, Zoho, Flipkart, Zomato
• Startups like Niramai (healthcare AI), CropIn (agri-AI), and more!

You Can Also Be...

A Student Entrepreneur:
Build and sell an app powered by ML—solve a real problem and launch your startup.

A Global Competitor:
Join contests like Technovation, AI World Cup, Kaggle for Kids, and Google Science Fair.

Illustration Prompt

Scene: A diverse group of teens at a "Career Expo" booth for ML. Each one is wearing a badge: ML Engineer, AI Artist, Ethical Hacker, Data Detective. A mentor guides them through a roadmap poster showing school → projects → college → careers.

Activity: "Design Your ML Career Card"

Draw a card with:

- Career name (like "Chatbot Designer")
- Skills needed
- What problems you'll solve
- Your ML tools
- Why it excites you

Display it in class or your study wall!

Career Toolkit: What Skills Do You Need?

Skill	Why It's Useful
Math & Logic	For pattern recognition, predictions
Coding Basics	For building tools or apps
Data Sense	For organizing and understanding data
Creativity	For new ideas, innovation, art
Communication	To explain your ML projects to others
Ethics	To build fair, kind, inclusive tech

Think & Reflect

- What kind of problems do you want to solve with ML?
- Which career excites you most?
- How can you use your strengths (math, art, communication) in ML?

Abeer's Quick Tip

You don't have to decide your ML career today. Focus on building skills—logical thinking, communication, and curiosity. Careers evolve, but strong foundations stay useful in every field.

Chapter Recap

• ML careers are growing fast across every industry
• You can start early with school subjects, online courses, and projects
• Careers include engineering, research, art, ethics, education, and more
• India is a global leader in AI jobs and opportunities
• Every strength—whether logic or creativity—has a role in ML

"Machine Learning is not just a subject—it's your superpower toolkit for tomorrow's world."

Chapter 12

The Future of ML

What's Next in the Smart World?

What Will the World Look Like in 2035?

Will we have flying taxis that avoid traffic jams using ML?
Will your school lessons be fully personalized by AI tutors?
Could doctors detect diseases before you even feel sick?
Machine Learning isn't just a tool for today—it's the technology of tomorrow. In this chapter, we'll explore what the future holds and how you can help shape it.
Let's look at the top trends, wild ideas, and real possibilities for the future of Machine Learning!

1. ML in Space – Beyond Planet Earth

ML is already helping scientists:

- Navigate Mars rovers
- Analyze space images for signs of life

• Predict satellite movement and collisions
• Monitor Earth's climate from space

Imagine This:
You build an ML model that studies photos from Jupiter's moons and detects signs of water.
You help ISRO track rocket stages in real-time using pattern prediction.
Space + ML = One giant leap for science

2. ML for Climate and Sustainability

One of the biggest uses of ML will be in solving Earth's problems.

Future Applications:
• Predict floods, droughts, and heatwaves
• Reduce electricity wastage using smart grids
• Analyze forest health with drone + ML combo
• Suggest eco-friendly routes to reduce pollution

India Examples:
• CropIn and SatSure use ML to help farmers with climate advice
• Swasthya Slate tracks pollution-linked illnesses
ML could help us heal the planet faster than we harm it.

3. ML + Human Brain – Smarter Together

Future systems won't just replace human thinking—they'll work with it.

Human-AI Collaboration:
• Doctors + ML = Early disease detection
• Teachers + ML = Personalized lessons
• Artists + ML = Infinite creativity
New roles like AI Coaches, AI Therapists, and AI Helpers for Seniors will emerge.

4. Education Revolution – Learning Gets Smarter

Tomorrow's schools may use ML for:

Feature	What It Does
AI Tutors	Explain tough topics based on your learning style
Skill Maps	Suggest your best-fit career
Smart Reports	Track learning trends, not just marks
Language Tools	Translate content into your mother tongue instantly

Students will learn what, why, and how—with the support of ML.

5. Ethics and Laws – Smarter, Kinder Tech

As ML becomes powerful, the world will need rules and guardians to:

- Protect privacy
- Avoid harmful bias
- Stop misinformation
- Prevent job loss and tech abuse

You might be part of India's first generation of AI Policy Makers—writing fair laws for the digital future.

6. Jobs of the Future – Get Ready!

Here are future jobs that didn't exist 10 years ago:

Future Role	What They Might Do
Climate ML Analyst	Use ML to stop pollution and plan green cities
AI Education Designer	Build smart courses using ML tutors
Robotic Health Coach	Help patients recover with ML-powered bots
Creative AI Writer	Use ML to write poems, comics, games
Bias Auditor	Check ML systems for unfair decisions

Many students will create jobs that don't even exist yet!

Illustration Prompt

A futuristic city scene showing students flying drones, ML-powered trash bins, climate dashboards, and AI tutors floating like holograms.

A poster reads: "Future Ready with ML!"

What Tools Might Exist in 10 Years?

- Brain-Machine Interfaces (like Neuralink)
- AI Art Partner apps that paint as you speak
- Real-time, global classroom translators
- ML-powered diplomacy tools to prevent conflict
- Drug discovery bots that reduce testing time by 90%

India's Role in the Global ML Future

- **India is a global ML hub, especially in:**
  - o FinTech (Digital payments, UPI)

o HealthTech (Aarogya Setu, Niramai)
o AgriTech (AI for crop monitoring)
o EduTech (BYJU'S, LEAD School)

• Government-backed programs like Digital India, Make in India, and AI for All are training lakhs of students.

The world's smartest tech may speak Hindi, Tamil, Marathi, or Assamese.

Think & Reflect

• What's one big problem you'd like to solve in the future using ML?
• If you could invent a tool for 2035, what would it do?
• How do we balance smart machines with kindness and fairness?

Career Spotlight

Future ML Creator – Future Leader
Even before graduating school, you can:

• Build climate or health projects
• Participate in Young AI Innovator awards
• Teach others in your community how ML works
• Start a blog or YouTube series on smart tech

The best ML creators will not just be smart… they'll be empathetic, ethical, and inclusive.

Activity: "ML in 2035" Vision Poster

Draw or design your version of the future:

• A smart classroom
• An ML-powered farm
• A robot librarian
• An AI-powered fashion stylist
• ML apps in your village or neighborhood

Stick your poster on your wall—and dream big!

Chapter Recap

• ML will be part of every future—from space to climate to school
• New careers and inventions will grow where ML and humans work together
• India is leading in responsible, inclusive ML development
• You don't just prepare for the future—you create it

"The future of ML isn't written in code — it's written in dreams, like yours."

Chapter 13

India & Machine Learning

The Big Picture

India's ML Journey – From Roots to Rise

When you think of Machine Learning, you may imagine Silicon Valley, big tech companies, and fancy labs.

But here's a fact:
India is one of the fastest-growing Machine Learning hubs in the world.
From small villages to smart cities, from crop fields to coding classrooms—ML is helping India solve real problems.

In this chapter, we'll explore:
• India's ML achievements
• Government initiatives
• Startups and innovators
• Challenges ahead

• How you can be part of India's ML future
Let's zoom out and see the big picture.

Real Problems, Real ML Solutions – Indian Style

Agriculture
• CropIn and SatSure use ML to predict harvest times and detect diseases using satellite data.
• Farmers use photo-based apps like Plantix to diagnose plant problems.

Healthcare
• Niramai uses ML for non-invasive breast cancer screening.
• Aarogya Setu helped track COVID-19 with contact tracing powered by ML.

Education
• Platforms like BYJU'S, Toppr, and LEAD School personalize learning using ML.
• Diksha App curates content based on student needs and languages.

Finance & Banking
• UPI and RBI's AI systems monitor transaction fraud in real time.
• Apps suggest personalized loans, budgets, and financial tips based on user data.

Transport & Traffic
• ML is being used in Bangalore and Hyderabad for smart traffic signals.
• Indian Railways uses predictive ML to reduce breakdowns.

IndiaStack – Our Digital Foundation

You've probably used Aadhaar, UPI, or DigiLocker. But did you know these are part of IndiaStack, a digital public infrastructure powered by ML?

Layer	ML Impact
Presenceless (Aadhaar)	Face, fingerprint, iris recognition
Paperless (DigiLocker)	Document classification & storage
Cashless (UPI)	Secure, real-time transactions with fraud detection
Consent Layer (Account Aggregator)	ML helps users share data safely with banks or services

IndiaStack proves that Machine Learning is not just for elites—it's for everyone.

Startups Making It Big with ML

Startup	What It Does
Niramai	Breast cancer detection using ML and thermal imaging
CropIn	ML for farmers—predicts weather, diseases, yield
SigTuple	ML for medical diagnostics in blood tests and X-rays
Arya.ai	Builds ML tools for banks and insurance
Qure.ai	Detects brain injuries from CT scans faster than humans

India is home to 1,000+ AI/ML startups, many solving real Indian problems.

Government Initiatives Powering ML in Schools

CBSE's AI Curriculum

• For Grades 6–12
• Covers basics of ML, ethical AI, and fun hands-on projects
• Includes modules on Teachable Machine, Scratch, and chatbot creation

Atal Innovation Mission (NITI Aayog)

• Atal Tinkering Labs (ATLs) provide tools and mentorship to create ML projects
• Students build climate tools, assistive bots, safety apps, and more
• ATL Marathons showcase India's youngest ML creators!

Digital India and AI for Youth

• Programs for students in rural and urban schools
• Free access to learning content
• Partnerships with companies like Intel, IBM, and Google

Illustration Prompt

Scene: A classroom in a small town. Students are working on laptops and posters. One screen shows "Soil Health App," another "ML Quiz Bot." A teacher writes on the board: "India's Future = Smart + Inclusive".

India's ML Challenges

While India is growing fast in ML, we also face challenges:

Challenge	Impact
Digital Divide	Some students lack internet or devices
Lack of Trained Teachers	Not all schools have AI/ML instructors
Language Barriers	Most ML tools are in English
Data Bias	Not enough Indian voices and faces in datasets
Privacy Concerns	Need stronger data protection laws

The Way Forward:

• Build ML tools in local languages
• Create low-data AI tools for low-internet areas
• Include more girls and rural youth in programs
• Pass laws that protect user privacy
ML in India must be inclusive, accessible, and responsible.

Think & Reflect

• What are three things you think ML could improve in your community or city?
• Do you think India's languages and cultures should be part of ML training? Why?
• How can we make sure everyone—not just techies—benefits from ML?

Career Spotlight: India's Future ML Leaders

Thousands of Indian teens are now:
• Building ML projects in school
• Joining state-level innovation challenges
• Publishing on GitHub, YouTube, or science fairs
• Teaching ML to younger kids in their villages
You could be next. Start small, think local—and solve real problems with ML.

Your Role in India's ML Future

You don't need to be a genius or billionaire. You just need:
• Curiosity to ask questions
• Compassion to solve real issues
• Commitment to keep learning
• Community spirit to teach and share
India's ML revolution needs artists, poets, coders, teachers, farmers, and thinkers. That means YOU.

Chapter Recap

• India is using ML in agriculture, health, education, and finance
• Initiatives like IndiaStack, ATLs, and CBSE AI curriculum support young learners
• Startups and students are solving real Indian challenges with ML
• Challenges like digital divide, language barriers, and bias still exist
• The future of ML in India must be inclusive, ethical, and localized

"India's ML revolution will not be imported—it will be invented by students like you."

Chapter 14

10 Myths About ML – Busted!

Myth vs. Reality – Let's Set the Record Straight

You've heard a lot about Machine Learning by now. It can power smart assistants, detect diseases, and even generate songs and pictures.

But… you've probably also heard scary or confusing things like:
• "It'll take over all our jobs!"
• "Only geniuses can understand it!"
• "ML is the same as AI, right?"
The truth? Most of what people think about ML is based on myths. In this chapter, we'll bust the 10 biggest myths about Machine Learning. Get ready for a reality check!

Myth 1: ML is Only for Coders and Computer Geniuses

Truth: ML is for everyone—including artists, students, and hobbyists.

Thanks to tools like Teachable Machine, MLforKids, and Scratch ML, even kids can train a machine to recognize patterns—without a single line of code.
Many Indian students in Grades 6 to 10 are already building ML-powered apps!

Myth 2: ML is the Same as AI

Truth: ML is just one part of AI.
ML is about learning from data.
AI is the bigger umbrella that includes learning, reasoning, planning, language understanding, and more.

Think of AI as the whole smart robot, and ML as its learning brain.

Myth 3: ML is 100% Accurate and Always Right

Truth: ML can make mistakes—especially if the data is bad.
If you train a model only on photos of cats, it may mislabel a dog.
ML systems are only as smart as the data you give them.

That's why testing, feedback, and improvement are important.

Myth 4: ML Will Replace All Human Jobs

Truth: ML may change jobs—but it also creates new ones.
Sure, some routine tasks may get automated.

But ML is also creating jobs like:
- AI Ethics Consultant
- Data Artist
- ML Coach
- AI Storyboard Designer

Future jobs will need humans + machines working together.

Myth 5: ML Can Think Like a Human

Truth: ML can't feel, imagine, or think like you.

ML is great at recognizing patterns and making predictions, but it doesn't have:
- Emotions
- Common sense
- Ethics or compassion

That's why we need humans to guide and correct ML systems.

Myth 6: ML Can Learn Everything on Its Own

Truth: ML needs tons of examples, feedback, and human help.

You must:
- Clean the data
- Label it correctly
- Choose the right model
- Train, test, and improve

ML is more like a student than a genius—it learns with practice and guidance.

Myth 7: ML Is Always Biased and Dangerous

Truth: ML can be fair and safe—if we build it responsibly.

Bias happens when:
- The training data is limited or unfair
- The labels reflect past discrimination

To fix this, we need:
- Diverse teams
- Ethical guidelines

• Regular audits
ML is not bad—it's the way we train and use it that matters.

Myth 8: ML Is All About Math and Coding

Truth: ML also needs creativity, curiosity, and empathy.

ML careers today include:
• ML artists who paint using data
• ML educators who simplify learning
• ML storytellers who explain smart tech
• Community builders who teach rural youth ML

There's room for everyone in the ML world—not just math nerds.

Myth 9: You Need Fancy Devices to Try ML

Truth: All you need is a basic phone or computer + internet.

Many ML tools work online and are:
• Free
• Beginner-friendly
• Supported by the government (like AI for Youth, Diksha App, ATL Labs)

Even your school project or science fair can include ML!

Myth 10: ML Is Only for Big Cities and Big Companies

Truth: ML is changing small towns and villages too.

From farmers using image-based crop diagnosis, to students in Ladakh building ML-powered solar trackers—ML is growing everywhere.
ML is not about your location. It's about your imagination.

Illustration Prompt

Two panels:
• Left: A child looks at a robot and thinks, “I’ll never understand ML.”
• Right: Same child smiling as they use Teachable Machine to make a model.

Caption: “Myth Busted. You can do ML too!”
Activity: "Truth Tracker"

Make a table like this:

Myth I Heard	What I Found Out
ML is only for adults	Even kids can use MLforKids!
ML will take all jobs	It’s creating new ones too!

Share it in your class bulletin board or ML club!

Think & Reflect

• What myths about ML had you believed before?
• Which myth was most surprising to bust?
• How can we spread truthful knowledge about ML in your school or community?

Career Spotlight

ML Awareness Educator
Teaches students, parents, and communities the truth about ML.

Helps people:

- Use ML safely
- Understand its benefits
- Stay alert about bias or fake claims

You can become a student ambassador in your school or online club!

Chapter Recap

Myth	Reality
ML is only for coders	It's for everyone
ML never makes mistakes	It can—if the data is flawed
ML will take all jobs	It'll create new, exciting ones
ML is just math	It's also about people and purpose

"Truth is power. When you understand ML, you're not just a user—you're a builder of the future."

Chapter 15

Checklist to Begin Your ML Journey

Ready, Set, Learn!

You've reached the final chapter of your beginner's journey into Machine Learning—and what an incredible journey it's been!

But here's the truth:
The real journey starts now—when YOU take action.
This chapter is your starter kit—a checklist of tools, mindsets, habits, and steps to help you confidently begin your Machine Learning adventure.

Let's go from curious reader to real-life ML creator. Are you ready?

1. Build Your Beginner's Toolkit

You don't need expensive gear. You just need a curious mind, an internet connection, and these free and simple tools:

Tool	Use
Teachable Machine	Create ML models with webcam or audio
ML for Kids	Build games/chatbots with ML + Scratch
MIT App Inventor	Make ML-powered mobile apps
QuickDraw	Understand image recognition ML
DALL·E	Create AI-generated images from text
CBSE AI Curriculum	Official modules for school students
Kaggle (beginner mode)	Try ML challenges and datasets

Pick one and start playing with it today—even 15 minutes counts!

2. Choose a Problem You Care About

ML isn't just for school marks—it's for solving real problems.

Ask yourself:
- What bugs you?
- What do people in your community need?
- How could technology help?

Example Ideas:
- A chatbot that answers climate questions
- A tool to help seniors remember tasks
- A game that detects your mood from your face
- A school quiz grader
- An ML-powered village guide in your local language

ML is most powerful when it has a heart.

3. Set Mini Goals (and Celebrate Them!)

Break your journey into small steps:

Week	Goal
Week 1	Explore Teachable Machine and train a simple model
Week 2	Watch 2 YouTube videos on ML basics
Week 3	Pick a project idea and sketch it
Week 4	Build version 1 and test with friends
Week 5	Share in school group or with a mentor

Celebrate each win—no matter how small!

4. Join a Learning Community

You don't have to do this alone. ML is more fun when shared.

Join or Create:
• A school AI/ML club
• Online forums like Google AI for Youth, Girls Who Code, or Kaggle for Beginners
• CBSE ATL or AI Showcase groups
• WhatsApp or Discord learning pods
Ask questions, share projects, encourage others. Together, you go farther.

5. Practice These Habits Weekly

Habit	Why It Matters
Ask Questions	ML is powered by curiosity
Keep a Learning Journal	Track your ideas, tools, and progress
Spot ML in Daily Life	Look for hidden ML around you
Play Creatively	Mix ML with art, games, storytelling
Explain ML to Others	Teaching helps you learn better too!

6. Keep This ML Learner's Code

Raise your hand (yes, right now!) and say:
"I may be young, but I'm not too early.
I will explore, learn, and create.
I will use Machine Learning to help, not harm.
I will include others.

And I will stay curious—always!"

Congratulations. You've just written your ML Code of Honor.

My Personalized ML Launch Checklist

Print this and tick as you go!
✓ I've tried a beginner ML tool (Teachable Machine / MLforKids)
✓ I've listed a real-life problem I want to solve
✓ I've drawn/sketched my project idea
✓ I've talked to a teacher or friend about ML
✓ I've joined or started an ML club or group
✓ I've completed one mini-project or challenge

✓ I've reflected on how I want to use ML ethically
✓ I've had FUN while learning!

Think & Reflect

- What do I want to create in the next 3 months using ML?
- Who can I team up with to learn together?
- How can I help others understand ML better?

Illustration Prompt

A kid standing on top of a small staircase labeled:
1. Ask Questions
2. Try ML Tools
3. Build a Project
4. Share & Teach
5. Grow!

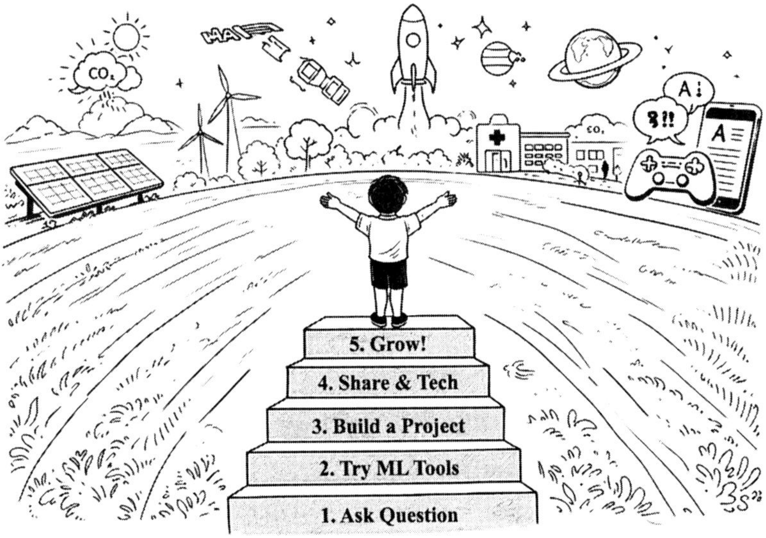

Behind them: a wide open field of possibilities—climate tech, space, healthcare, games, language apps, and more.

Career Spotlight

ML Pathfinder

You may not be an expert yet—but you're clearing the way for others. Every question you ask, every model you try, every problem you care about—brings us one step closer to an ML-powered future that's fair, helpful, and human.

Abeer's Quick Tip

Consistency matters more than intensity. Even 20 minutes a week exploring ML tools will teach you more than one intense weekend of trying to master everything. Learning is a marathon, not a hackathon.

Chapter Recap

- You can begin your ML journey today—with free tools and real problems
- Choose mini goals, form habits, and build projects step by step
- Join learning groups and share your voice
- Stay curious, be ethical, and have fun
- You're not just a learner—you're a builder of India's smart tomorrow

"Start where you are. Use what you have. Learn all you can. Create something great."

GLOSSARY

Term	Definition
Algorithm	A set of rules or instructions a computer follows to solve a problem. Like a recipe for solving tasks.
Artificial Intelligence (AI)	The ability of machines to do tasks that usually require human intelligence—like understanding language or recognizing faces.
Bias (in ML)	When a machine learning model shows unfair behavior because it was trained on unbalanced or incorrect data.
Chatbot	A computer program that simulates conversation with users, often used in websites or messaging apps.
Classification	Sorting data into categories. For example, label-ing emails as 'spam' or 'not spam.'
Clustering	Grouping similar things together based on their features, without knowing labels.
Data	Information collected in numbers, text, images, or sounds that computers use to learn.
Dataset	A large collection of data used to train and test machine learning models.
Deep Learning	A type of machine learning that uses layers of algorithms (like a brain) to learn from complex data, like images or speech.
Ethics (in AI/ML)	The rules and values that guide how AI should be developed and used safely and fairly.
Feature	A piece of information or characteristic used by a model to make decisions. For example, height and weight can be features in a health model.

Kaggle	An online platform where people can practice data science, compete in challenges, and learn ML.
Label	The answer or outcome a model is supposed to learn, like "cat" or "dog" in an image.
Machine Learning (ML)	A way for computers to learn from data and improve over time without being told exactly what to do.
Model	The final product of training—an ML program that can make predictions or decisions.
Neural Network	A system inspired by the human brain, made of interconnected nodes, used in deep learning to understand patterns.
Overfitting	When a model is too focused on the training data and doesn't work well on new or unseen data.
Pattern Recognition	The process of detecting trends or similarities in data.
Prediction	What a model says will happen based on new input data. Like guessing a movie rating based on past behavior.
Reinforcement Learning	A type of ML where the model learns by trying and getting rewards or penalties—like training a pet.
Supervised Learning	ML where the model is trained with both input and correct output (like flashcards).
Teachable Machine	A free tool by Google that lets you train ML models using pictures, sounds, or poses.
Unsupervised Learning	ML where the model tries to find patterns without being given the correct answers.

BOOK SUMMARY

What Is This Book About?

This book is a beginner-friendly guide for preteens and teenagers (Grades 6–12) who want to understand Machine Learning—the technology behind smart apps, robots, and AI.

It uses simple stories, analogies, activities, and real-life examples to make Machine Learning fun and easy to learn!

What Will You Learn?

You'll learn:

- What Machine Learning is and how it's different from AI
- How ML works (with data, patterns, and models)
- The 3 main types of ML: Supervised, Unsupervised, Reinforcement
- How ML is used in your everyday life—from Face ID to shopping ads
- Tools you can use to try ML (like Teachable Machine and Scratch ML)
- Cool projects you can build—no coding needed!
- The ethics of ML—what's fair, safe, and responsible use
- ML in India's development (Digital India, UPI, Aadhaar)
- Career paths and opportunities in the ML and AI industry
- How YOU can start your ML journey today

What Makes This Book Special?

- Friendly tone like a mentor—not a textbook
- Cartoon-style illustration prompts for each concept
- Real Indian examples and local use cases
- "Think & Reflect" and "Career Spotlight" boxes
- Step-by-step starter checklist for your ML journey
- Supports NEP 2020's vision of 21st-century skills

Who Is This Book For?

- Curious students between 10–18 years old
- Teachers and schools introducing AI/ML in classrooms
- Parents who want to support digital learning at home
- Clubs, hobby groups, and AI-for-Youth programs

Final Message to Readers:

"You don't need to be a genius to learn ML.
You just need to be curious, ethical, and brave enough to start."

The future is not just for experts—it's for explorers like YOU.